Historic Places of Early America

Historic Places
of Early America

David M. Brownstone
Irene M. Franck

ALADDIN BOOKS
Macmillan Publishing Company • New York

Aladdin Books
Macmillan Publishing Company
866 Third Avenue, New York, NY 10022
Collier Macmillan Canada, Inc.

First Aladdin Books edition 1989

Printed in the United States of America

A hardcover edition of *Historic Places of Early America* is available from Atheneum,
Macmillan Publishing Company.

10 9 8 7 6 5 4 3 2 1

Library of Congress Cataloging-in-Publication Data

Brownstone, David M.
Historic places of early America/by David Brownstone, Irene Franck.—1st Aladdin
Books ed.
        p.   cm.
Includes index.
Summary: Describes places where early American history was made, from Indian and
Viking settlements through the Revolution.
1. Historic sites—United States—Juvenile literature. 2. Historic sites—Canada—Juvenile
literature. 3. United States—History—Colonial period, ca. 1600-1775—Juvenile literature.
4. United States—History—Revolution. 1775-1783—Juvenile literature. 5. Canada—
History—To 1763 (New France)—Juvenile literature. [1. Historic buildings. 2. Historic
sites. 3. United States—History.] I. Franck, Irene M. II. Title.
E159.B894   1989b
973—dc 19   88-39238   CIP · AC
ISBN 0-689-71234-0

Contents

Preface

In this book, you will find dozens of fascinating places from early America. Here are Santa Fe and Plymouth Rock, Williamsburg and Salem, Carmel Mission and Independence Hall, St. Augustine's Castillo de San Marcos and Quebec's Plains of Abraham, Valley Forge and Cumberland Gap—and a great many more. Here, too, you will find stories of the many peoples who shaped early America—among them the Anasazi of the Canyon de Chelly, the Vikings of L'Anse aux Meadows, the Russians of Sitka, the Spanish of El Morro, the French of Grand Pré, the Jews of Newport, and the British of Jamestown.

In *Historic Places of Early America*, you can both see and read about the places where much of America's early history was made, from the settlements in early times to just after the American Revolution. Both words and pictures are meant to give the flavor of each place, as well as tell why and how the place became special and important. The pictures, in full color, are drawn from all over North America and beyond, from Puerto Rico to Alaska, from San Diego to Newfoundland. Throughout we have focused on places where there is, in fact, something to *see*—and perhaps later to visit. The places are grouped in alphabetical order. To make everything easy to find, a full index is provided at the back of the book.

We hope that you will enjoy *Historic Places of Early America* and that reading the book will make you want to visit as many of these places as you can.

The Bunker Hill Monument towers over old Boston.

Bunker Hill

The American Revolution had begun with the encounters between the colonists and the British at Lexington and Concord, in April of 1775. Two months later, American troops encircled Boston. There, at the Battle of Bunker Hill, American and British troops fought the first major battle of the war.

Actually, it should have been called the Battle of Breed's Hill. Both hills are across the Charles River from Boston, and on June 16, Colonel William Prescott's American troops set out to fortify Bunker's Hill (the hill's correct name). It is uncertain why, but for some reason they decided to fortify Breed's Hill instead. Prescott started with about 1,200 men and was later reinforced by more.

The next day, the Americans were attacked by about 2,200 British troops, led by General William Howe. The first attack, against the left side of the American line, was thrown back with heavy British losses. Then the British attacked along the whole line. That attack was thrown back with even heavier losses.

Finally, the British attacked for a third time. They broke through the American line and took Breed's Hill, forcing the Americans to retreat. The British, who had suffered large losses, did not follow.

In this first major battle of the American Revolution, almost half of the British—over 1,000 out of 2,200 men—were killed or wounded in action. Less than half that number of Americans—about 450 in all—were killed, wounded, or taken prisoner. Although the Americans lost the battle, it showed that the new American army could successfully fight the experienced British regular army. Boston continued to be encircled by the Americans. The British finally left it, by sea, in 1776. Today a monument—with a beautiful view of Boston—marks the site of the Battle of Bunker Hill.

California Missions

California's Carmel Mission recalls the days of Father Junípero Serra.

San Diego Bay was discovered in 1542 by Juan Rodríguez Cabrillo, only fifty years after Columbus first sailed to America. Yet it took Spain over two hundred years more to plant settlements at San Diego and farther north in California. For Spain, California seemed a faraway, poor place, and hardly worth bothering about.

What little Spanish settlement there was in California was mainly the accomplishment of one Spanish explorer-priest and his followers. He was Father Junípero Serra, who in 1769 began building what became a string of twenty-one missions all the way from San Diego to north of San Francisco. Their purpose was to convert the Indians to Christianity.

In the spring of 1769, a party of soldiers and priests headed north out of Mexico toward Alta (Upper) California, as it was then called. A second party went north by ship. After months of traveling, both parties reached San Diego Bay. There, Father Serra built his first California mission, the Mission San Diego de Alcalá. As they had throughout the New World, the Spaniards used enslaved local Indians to do the building.

There was an Indian revolt in San Diego in 1775, but the mission survived and prospered. Soon, it was one of the richest of all the California missions. As it was the first mission, too, it has often been called the Mother Mission.

After building San Diego Mission, Father Serra's party traveled north along the coast, mostly following Indian coastal trails. They walked hundreds of miles, making about six miles a day on good days and less in very rough country. Finally, the Spanish priests and soldiers reached Monterey Bay. There, in June 1770, Father Serra—again using enslaved local Indians to do the work—built his second California mission. He named it Mission San Carlos Borromeo del Rio Carmelo. At the same time and at the same place, the soldiers in the party, commanded by Captain Gaspar de Portolá, built a fort, which they called a presidio.

The next year Father Serra moved down the coast, to a few miles south of what is now Carmel. There he built another mission, which he gave the same name as the one in Monterey. This mission became known as the Home Mission, as it was his headquarters for all the rest of his life. Father Serra is buried on the grounds of the mission.

Father Serra went on to build many more missions. He died in 1784, and was buried at the

The San Diego Mission, built first, was known as the Mother Mission.

Carmel Mission. His work was then carried on by other priests, who ultimately built the balance of the twenty-one California missions.

In 1835, the Mexican government declared the missions no longer churches, at which point most Indians left them. Soon, the mission buildings were neglected, and began to fall apart. But in our time the California missions are seen as a key part of the history of early California. Many, including San Diego Mission, the Mission San Luís Rey de Francia at Oceanside, and the Santa Barbara Mission, have been restored for the interest and enjoyment of hundreds of thousands of visitors every year.

3

Canyon de Chelly

This Anasazi dwelling under a cliff overhang is called the Mummy Cave.

Canyon de Chelly in Arizona is a great valley filled with the ruins of old Indian towns. You can see ruins like them throughout the Southwest. They were built long ago—some of them a thousand years ago, long before Columbus discovered America. When the Spanish arrived, they called these places pueblos—the Spanish word for "towns." And they are still known as pueblos today.

Several peoples lived in the Southwest in early times. But the main town builders were the people called the Anasazi. Their name means "the Old Ones." Starting about thirteen hundred years ago, the Anasazi built many towns and villages, including those at Canyon de Chelly. There they lived in what we would today call large apartment houses, or condominiums, or co-ops. Some of the huge buildings had many hundreds of rooms. For example, there is one building at Chaco Canyon, in New Mexico, called Pueblo Bonito. It is over five stories high and has over eight hundred rooms. Probably more than a thousand people lived there.

In their towns, the Anasazi also built networks of roads, and large underground places of religious worship called Great Kivas. This was also very dry country, so the Anasazi dug large irrigation systems that brought much-needed water to their farms and homes.

The Anasazi built many of their towns in places that were easy to defend against their enemies. That is why so many of their pueblos are found on cliffs, in the mouths of big caves, in canyons, and very high out on the flat tops of the huge rock formations called mesas. In those locations, many of the towns must have been extremely difficult to build, calling for great skill, patience, and hard work.

In early times, the Anasazi and most other peoples of the Southwest made their living by farming. They were generally peaceful, but long before the Spanish came, they were attacked by new groups of Indians, coming from the northern plains. Among these more warlike peoples were the Navajos and the Apaches. In fact, the name Apache comes from the language of the Anasazi Indians and means "enemy." The Apaches and Navajos soon settled in the Southwest alongside the other, earlier peoples.

After about 1300, the Anasazi began to move out of many of their towns. We do not know why for sure. Even so, when the Spanish came to America, many Indian peoples, including some Anasazi, still lived in towns throughout the Southwest. Because they were town dwellers, the Spanish called all of them Pueblo Indians. Some Indians still live in some of these towns in the Southwest. Acoma Pueblo, in New Mexico, is the oldest occupied place in the United States. It was built about eight hundred years ago, three hundred years before Columbus sailed to America.

Throughout the Southwest, archeologists and historians have found and studied hundreds of Anasazi ruins. These old towns supply knowledge of some of America's most skilled and advanced Indian peoples. Many tourists, too, are drawn to the pueblos, especially to the strikingly beautiful Canyon de Chelly.

Ruins of old Anasazi dwellings lie deep in Canyon de Chelly's Mummy Cave.

Carpenters Hall

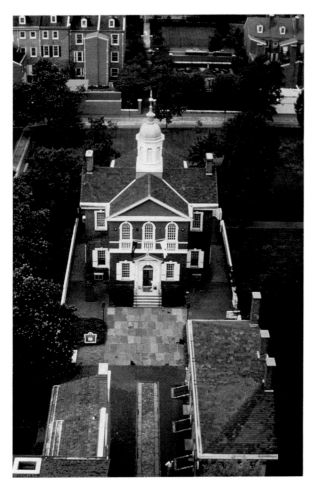

America's first Continental Congress met here, at Carpenters Hall, in 1775.

The years before the American Revolution were a time of trouble in Britain's American colonies. Patrick Henry in Virginia, Samuel Adams in Boston, and dozens of others spoke out against the British government and its unfair treatment of the colonies. Throughout the colonies, there were larger and larger public meetings, and more and more action taken to force the British to respond to the colonists' grievances.

Here, at Carpenters Hall, in Philadelphia, is one place where the American colonists started down the road to revolution—the road that would lead to Concord, Bunker Hill, Valley Forge, Yorktown, and freedom.

At Carpenters Hall, on September 5, 1775, the first Continental Congress met. Every American colony but Georgia sent delegates to the Congress. At the start, the fifty-six delegates disagreed on many things. Some were revolutionaries, who wanted to move toward independence. Others were moderates, who wanted somehow to work out problems while staying part of Britain.

The revolutionaries, led by Samuel Adams, won the day. This first Continental Congress called for the formation of revolutionary committees throughout the American colonies. So began the process of separation from Britain. The Continental Congress passed a strong list of demands, and they decided not to buy British goods until those demands were met. Most of the moderates went along, then and on into the Revolution, which began less than a year later, in April 1776, at Lexington and Concord.

Today, Carpenters Hall is part of Philadelphia's Independence National Historical Park, along with Independence Hall, the Liberty Bell, and many other historic places.

Castillo de San Marcos

The Castillo de San Marcos defended St. Augustine from attack by sea.

The Castillo de San Marcos is a huge old Spanish fort in northern Florida that once guarded St. Augustine, the oldest city in the United States. The walls of the fort are thirty feet high and up to twelve feet thick. They are built of coquina, a local stone made of small crushed seashells. Started in 1672, the Castillo de San Marcos was designed by Spanish engineers. Enslaved Florida Indians did the actual building, over a period of almost twenty-five years.

The city of St. Augustine was founded in 1565 by Spanish explorer Pedro Menéndez de Avilés. It was a northern strongpoint of Spain's American empire. At one time, that empire extended thousands of miles, all the way from Florida to the southern tip of South America. From forts like the Castillo de San Marcos, the Spanish fought for over two hundred years for control of the Caribbean Sea, Central America, and Florida.

From St. Augustine, Spanish fleets controlled the whole northern Florida coast from the late 1500s to the mid-1700s. From there the Spanish also raided British settlers in the Carolinas and Georgia.

But St. Augustine was attacked, too. Sir Francis Drake took and burned the city in 1586. British pirate John Davis did the same in 1668, as did later raiders from the Carolinas. There were also other attacks on the city, by Indians, pirates, and British troops. The British took control of St. Augustine in 1763, but the Spanish took it back in 1783, and held on to it until 1821, when they sold Florida to the United States.

From then on, the Castillo de San Marcos and St. Augustine were part of the United States. But the fort's bloody story was not yet done. The United States Army fought Florida's Seminole Indians from there in the 1830s. During the Seminole War, the Seminoles surprised a party of 139 American soldiers at the Castillo de San Marcos, and killed all but four of them. The Seminoles retreated into Florida's swamps and were never completely defeated.

The Castillo de San Marcos was also often used as a prison. The British held Americans there during the American Revolution. The Americans held army deserters there during the Spanish-American War. Renamed Fort Marion, it was used as a prison for Seminoles early in the 1800s. Later, it was a prison for Indian peoples captured in the Southwest, including Apaches, Cheyennes, Comanches, Kiowas, and others.

Today, the Castillo de San Marcos is a national monument, and St. Augustine is visited by thousands of travelers every year.

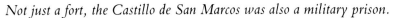

Not just a fort, the Castillo de San Marcos was also a military prison.

Christiansted

Christiansted was the old slave market center on St. Croix Island.

Christiansted is on St. Croix Island, one of the Virgin Islands, in the Caribbean Sea. It is the only place actually discovered by Columbus that is now part of the United States.

Columbus discovered the island in 1493. He named it Santa Cruz, which is Spanish for "Holy Cross." Only a few European settlers and some pirates lived on Santa Cruz after Spanish forces destroyed the native Arawak and Carib peoples. And in 1650 the Spanish also drove all other Europeans off the island. But although Spain claimed the island, no European country really held it until much later.

Shortly after the Spanish drove away the other Europeans, the French drove out the Spanish. They also changed the island's name, to the present-day St. Croix—French for "Holy Cross." But there were still very few settlers, as most of the French eventually resettled in Haiti.

Then, in 1733, Denmark took over St. Croix.

The Danes' main settlement on the island was Christiansted. Using Black African slaves, the Danes produced a great deal of sugar and some cotton for export to other countries. They also traded in slaves. Christiansted's slave market was one of the largest in the New World, until Denmark outlawed the slave trade in 1803. But the Danes kept the slaves they already had, and only after many slave revolts did the Danes finally free their slaves, in 1848.

Meanwhile, both the sugar industry and the population of St. Croix dropped sharply. In 1917, the United States bought the Virgin Islands from Denmark. Most of the people of the islands today are the descendants of Black African slaves brought in to produce sugar.

Christiansted National Historic Site is part of the waterfront of the old Danish town. It includes Fort Christiansted, the Old Danish Customhouse, and several other historic buildings.

Cumberland Gap

Cumberland Gap, a pass through the southern Appalachian Mountains, is the only really accessible way through the mountains for many hundreds of miles. Before the new settlers came, the pass was part of a very old network of trails, running on both sides of and across the mountains. The local Indians called this network the Warriors Path. Frontiersman Daniel Boone and those who traveled with him later created what came to be known as Wilderness Road. Hundreds of thousands of pioneers traveled the Wilderness Road, heading for Kentucky and the lands beyond.

The early English settlers, living east of the mountains, did not know about the pass until Thomas Walker discovered it in 1750. He went west through the mountains into Kentucky, through a pass he called Cave Gap. Later the name was changed to Cumberland Gap.

By the early 1770s, a few pioneers, including Daniel Boone, began to move through Cumberland Gap into Kentucky. Boone spent two years exploring in Kentucky, but tried and failed to lure other settlers there.

Then, early in 1775, Thomas Henderson met the leaders of the Cherokee nation at Sycamore Shoals. There, he "bought" from the Cherokees twenty million acres of land in Kentucky for a small amount of money and a few thousand pounds of trade goods. The Cherokees did not exactly own the land they sold. In fact, it was mostly Shawnee land, which the Cherokees, Shawnees, and other Indian peoples had been fighting over for a long time. But Henderson bought the Cherokee claim to the land. He then sent Daniel Boone and thirty axmen to clear a road good enough for settlers' wagons to pass through Cumberland Gap and into Kentucky.

That the axmen did, and in only ten days, for it was actually quite easy to follow the old Warriors Path into Kentucky. The frontiersmen were attacked by Shawnees on the other side of the mountains, but fought them off. A few weeks later, they reached the Kentucky River, over two hundred miles farther into Kentucky, where they waited for reinforcements. This time, Boone succeeded in settling Kentucky, attracting people to his new town, called Boonesboro. Other Kentucky settlements soon followed.

Settlement of Kentucky slowed down greatly during the American Revolution, as the pioneers had to fight hard just to survive. After the war, though, thousands of new settlers began to pour through Cumberland Gap. Some went even farther, out to the Mississippi River. The new United States was growing. Soon millions of pioneers were on their way west, on the Wilderness Road and the other great paths west across America to the Pacific.

After the Revolutionary War, pioneers poured through Cumberland Gap.

El Morro

The old Spanish fortress El Morro protected San Juan, Puerto Rico.

At San Juan, Puerto Rico, the huge old Spanish fortress of El Morro still looks out to sea, as it has for centuries. The great explorer Ponce de León founded the first Spanish colony on the island of Puerto Rico in 1609. From there he sailed north to discover Florida.

The Spanish, who held Puerto Rico for over three hundred years, began building this fort in the late 1530s. They named it Castillo de San Felipe del Morro—Spanish for "Castle of St. Philip of the Headland." It was well named, for it stands on a hill 140 feet above the sea. From there, its cannons commanded the entrance to the harbor, protecting the town of San Juan and its gold and silver, which was stored there waiting for the Spanish treasure fleets that would take it to Spain.

Others came for that gold and silver, too. One of them was English sea captain Francis Drake, who laid siege to El Morro in 1595 with twenty-three ships and an army of three thousand men. But El Morro, then only partly built and defended by only one thousand men, repelled him. Three years later, George Clifford's English army arrived and noted that while El Morro's cannons faced out to sea, the fort was unprotected from the rear. Clifford attacked from the land and won. The English did not stay, though. Disease struck them and they had to retreat, leaving Puerto Rico in the hands of Spain.

No one ever took El Morro after that. Dutch and British fleets came against it in later centuries, but the fort and its defenders fought them off. Even in 1898, Admiral William Sampson's American fleet could not take the fort. In the end, however, Spain lost the Spanish-American War, so Puerto Rico became part of the United States.

At San Juan there are other old Spanish landmarks besides El Morro. Ponce de León's home, La Casa Blanca ("The White House"), still stands. It was built for his family in 1525, and was part of the family's property for over two centuries, until 1779.

Here, too, are many other forts and walls, all built to protect San Juan from its many invaders. One of the largest of these forts is the Castillo de San Cristóbal, high on a hill overlooking the city. It was built in the mid-1600s. Another is the Caballero de San Miguel, a big, two-story cannon platform. A third is a tiny fort of only fifty square feet, across the harbor from El Morro. It provided still another platform for cannons defending the harbor and city. At one point during Spanish control there was also a massive wall built all around the city, protecting San Juan from invaders coming from the land side, as the English had done.

Today, El Morro and the other old Spanish forts and city walls of San Juan are all part of the San Juan National Historic Site.

The guns of El Morro all faced out to sea.

Faneuil Hall

Boston's Faneuil Hall is often called the Cradle of Liberty.

In the years before the start of the American Revolution, American colonists began to resist British rule. Much of that growing resistance was centered in Boston. It was no accident that the Revolution began in Lexington and Concord, near Boston. For Boston was at the heart of the fight for American freedom.

That is why Faneuil Hall, in downtown Boston, has so often been called the Cradle of Liberty. In Faneuil Hall, Boston citizens met again and again to protest British actions and then British rule.

As early as 1765, ten years before the Revolution, colonists meeting at Faneuil Hall protested the British Stamp Act, a law that hurt Boston's trade. In 1770, large meetings here condemned the Boston Massacre, during which British soldiers had fired into a crowd of colonists, killing five of them. Here, in 1772, Samuel Adams formed the first Committee of Correspondence. These committees led to the later Continental Congress, which finally decided to break away from British rule. And on December 16, 1773, a crowd of thousands outside Faneuil Hall supported protesters who were dressed like Indians. These "Indians," among them Paul Revere, boarded English ships in Boston and threw their cargo of tea into the harbor. This famous Boston Tea Party was one of the main events leading to the Revolution.

Faneuil Hall was built in 1742, almost destroyed by fire in 1761, and then rebuilt. It is named after Peter Faneuil, a rich Boston merchant who gave it to the city. In the mid-nineteenth century, before the Civil War, Faneuil Hall was often used for antislavery meetings.

Federal Hall

Here, at Federal Hall, George Washington became the first president of the United States.

After the American Revolution, there was still much work to be done. A new nation had been born. Now Americans had to form their own government—and that was not at all easy. Some Americans, including George Washington, saw the need for a strong new central government. But many others did not trust a strong central government. They wanted power to stay mainly with the state governments.

Washington was by far the most respected leader in the new United States. He had led his country through the war. Now he continued to lead it in its early days as a new nation, first as the president of the Constitutional Convention in Philadelphia, in 1787. This convention produced the United States Constitution, which made some very basic freedoms the right of every American. There, too, Washington was unanimously elected the first president of the United States.

Federal Hall, on Wall Street in New York City, is where Washington was first inaugurated—that is, officially became president. Here, on April 30, 1789, he took his first oath of office. New York had been the nation's capital since the end of the Revolution. It remained so until Congress moved to Philadelphia a year later. The federal government moved to Washington ten years later, in 1800. Actually, the old Federal Hall building no longer exists. But the building that replaced it serves as a museum and a reminder that here George Washington became the first president of the United States.

Fort Necessity

Modern "soldiers" recreate Washington's experience at Fort Necessity.

At Fort Necessity, in 1754, George Washington fought his first battle—and suffered his first defeat. The fort was in western Pennsylvania, near the forks of the Ohio, where the Monongahela and Allegheny rivers meet at what is now Pittsburgh.

There was no city at the forks of the Ohio then—or for that matter anywhere in western Pennsylvania. But there was Fort Duquesne, built by the French to control this great crossroads on the route west. There was no United States, either, for it was still twenty-two years before the American Revolution. At that point George Washington was a lieutenant colonel in the British army, leading a force of nearly three hundred Virginians. Their aim was to take the forks of the Ohio region from the French. At Great Meadows, Washington and his men met and defeated a small French scouting party, after

which the men built a small temporary fort that Washington named Fort Necessity.

But the French returned, this time with a force twice the size of Washington's Virginians. The French attacked the fort and took it in less than a day. Washington surrendered, and he and his soldiers were allowed to return to Virginia.

This was Washington's first real battle. It also marked the beginning of the final, seven-year-long war between Great Britain and France for control of North America. A year later, a British army led by General Edward Braddock was massacred near Fort Necessity by the French and their allies. Washington was there, too, covering the British retreat with his American soldiers. It was in these battles that Washington developed into the soldier who was to lead the American Revolution.

Fort Ross

Most of the Old World explorers and settlers came to America from the east, across the Atlantic. But the Russians came from the west, across the Bering Strait, the narrow water passage between Siberia and Alaska. While Daniel Boone was heading west through Kentucky, Russian explorers and traders were moving south from Alaska.

Fort Ross, in northern California, was as far south as the Russian settlers came, though Russian explorers had moved further south as early as the time that Father Junípero Serra and other Spanish explorers and settlers had been moving north. Its original name was not Fort Ross. The Russians called it Fort Stawianski. But the Spanish, who held southern and central California at that time, called it El Fuerte de los Russos—that is, "The Fort of the Russians." Later, Americans shortened it to "Fort Ross."

And that is the name we know it by today.

The fort certainly shows its Russian American heritage, with its dome and its seven-sided blockhouse. When it was first built in 1812, it was a very strong fort, with a four-hundred-man garrison and fifty cannons. Russian trappers hunted sea otter out of Fort Ross. Russian farmers settled in northern California, protected by the fort and its soldiers. But the sea otter supply soon gave out, and the Russian farmers did not do very well in northern California.

More important, the British and Americans strongly opposed the Russian presence there. In the end, the Russians decided to leave California. In 1841 they sold Fort Ross to John Sutter—at whose mill gold was discovered a few years later—and left the region. Soon the Russians left Alaska, as well.

California's Fort Ross is the old "Fort of the Russians."

Fort Ticonderoga

During the long series of British-French wars for control of North America before the American Revolution, Fort Ticonderoga was a great prize to be won. That is because of its location, just north of Lake George and south of Lake Champlain, in what is now New York State. The French wanted the fort because it could be used as a base for invading British lands further south. The British wanted it as a base for an invasion of French Canada. And each side wanted it as a defense against the other.

The French were the first to build a fort here. They named it Fort Vaudreuil, and later Fort Carillon. The British, seeing what a threat the fort was, attacked it in 1758 with a strong army. They were beaten back by General Louis Montcalm's French forces, but a year later, General Jeffrey Amherst's British army attacked the fort and proved too strong for the French, who retreated. Before they left, however, they blew up part of the fort.

After taking the fort, the British repaired it, and renamed it Fort Ticonderoga. From there, the British could defend the Hudson Valley and prepare to invade Canada. As it turned out, though, the main attack on French Canada was made from the sea, down the St. Lawrence River. It was led by General James Wolfe, and ended with the battle on Quebec's Plains of Abraham.

During the American Revolution, Fort Ticonderoga also passed back and forth between the British and American forces. It finally fell to the American army after its victory at nearby Saratoga, in 1777.

Fort Ticonderoga was a key site in the battle for North America.

Fraunces Tavern

George Washington said farewell to his officers at Fraunces Tavern.

Fraunces Tavern is the oldest surviving building on the island of Manhattan, in New York City. It was built in 1719 and made into a tavern in 1763. In the years before the American Revolution, it was a popular meeting place for such revolutionary groups as the Sons of Liberty, and it stayed open during the Revolution, even during the British army's occupation of New York City.

The Revolutionary War really ended at the Battle of Yorktown, in 1781. But the Americans, French, and British could not agree on peace terms until two years later, in 1783. Until then, George Washington and his officers could not formally lay down their arms. A peace treaty was finally worked out, and after eight long years, George Washington and the officers of the Continental army were able to put down their weapons.

Here, at Fraunces Tavern, on December 4, 1783, George Washington said good-bye to his officers. At the end of his farewell speech, he asked them all to "come and take me by the hand," and hugged each in turn. Then he walked the short distance to the ferry at the tip of Manhattan and went by boat to New Jersey. From there, he went to Annapolis, Maryland, and officially resigned as commander in chief.

Washington's years of service to his country were far from over, though. Soon the country's leader in war became its leader in peace, and its first president.

Grand Portage

Early fur traders carried their canoes overland at Grand Portage.

Long before frontiersmen like Daniel Boone began to explore westward, French explorers and traders went deep into the heartland of North America. From Montreal, explorers like Samuel de Champlain, Robert La Salle, and Pierre La Vérendrye followed swift, shallow rivers and traveled across many lakes to penetrate deep into the Midwest and far West.

These early French explorers were called voyageurs, a French word for "voyager" or "traveler." They and their crews usually traveled in the light, strong birchbark canoes long used by the local Indians. A birchbark canoe twenty to twenty-five feet long could move swiftly along a stream only a few inches deep—even though it was loaded with people, supplies, and trade goods.

Rather than a single waterway to follow, there were hundreds of waterways going west. Often, the voyageurs had to carry their canoes and supplies overland for miles, from one waterway to another. Two voyageurs could carry a birchbark canoe, while the others would carry the supplies. The French called that kind of overland walk between waterways a portage, a word that is still used by canoeists today, meaning a "carrying" or "transporting."

Grand Portage, a nine-mile portage between waterways in northern Minnesota, was shown to La Vérendrye by local guides on his way west in 1731. For about seventy years after that, this portage was the best way to travel east or west in the very difficult terrain of this part of northern North America. The passage was heavily used by trappers, traders, missionaries, and soldiers—and also by the few settlers who moved into western Canada that early. Later, Grand Portage became part of the United States, after which most Canadian travelers took east-west routes further north.

Today, an early fort has been rebuilt at Grand Portage National Monument.

Grand Pré

On July 28, 1755, something happened at Grand Pré that was to catch at the conscience of the Canadian people for two hundred years. The importance of the event spread beyond Canada, too, and caused Henry Wadsworth Longfellow to write one of the greatest of American poems.

The poem is *Evangeline*. It is about the separation of two French lovers, Evangeline and Gabriel, who then spent all their lives searching for each other. They were separated from each other when the British decided to expel all the French not only from Grand Pré but also from the whole region of Acadia. At the time, Acadia —which is called Nova Scotia today—was a French province. The British took Acadia from the French and insisted that the French people of Acadia take the oath of allegiance to Britain. But the French Acadians refused. In the end, the British expelled most Acadians from their homeland, forcing six thousand men, women, and children aboard ships bound for other British colonies. Some Acadians escaped and fought the British. Some went to French-speaking Louisiana and stayed in what would later become the United States. Some, years later, found their way home to Acadia, by then renamed Nova Scotia.

Grand Pré was the largest village of French Acadia. It was there that the order of expulsion was read. Today, it is the site of Grand Pré National Historical Park.

Evangeline *is a symbol of the tragedy of Grand Pré.*

Huronia

The Sainte-Marie Among the Hurons mission is recreated at Huronia.

Until 1649, the area around Huronia, in Canada's province of Ontario, was the home of the Huron League, a large group of Indian peoples. Lake Huron, one of the five Great Lakes, is named after these peoples. These Indians were related to the powerful Iroquois, who lived just south of them. Like the Iroquois, the Hurons lived in longhouses. They were farmers, raising such crops as corn, squash, and beans, as well as tobacco. They also hunted and traded in furs. In fact, they were part of the great fur-trading chain that went from their land all the way east to Quebec—and from there across the sea to Europe.

Many of Canada's early western explorers were Catholic missionaries who moved west from Quebec to try to convert the Indian peoples to Christianity. At Huronia itself Catholic Jesuit priests in 1626 built a small mission and fort they named Sainte-Marie. The mission at Huronia housed Ontario's first Catholic religious shrine, its first hospital, and its first pharmacy.

But the priests arrived at a time when the Iroquois to the south were attacking the weaker Hurons, whom they almost destroyed by 1649. Because of the trouble, the missionaries decided to leave, and burned Sainte-Marie. During their escape the Iroquois killed several of the priests, who were later made saints by the Catholic Church. After the wars with the Iroquois only a few hundred Hurons survived. Some moved east to Quebec, and the rest went west.

Huronia, in what is now Midland, Ontario, is a monument to those missionaries and to the Huron people. Today you can visit a reconstruction of the early mission there, named Sainte-Marie Among the Hurons. The town also has a reconstruction of a Huron village of the 1600s.

Independence Hall and the Liberty Bell

We hold these truths to be self-evident, that all men are created equal, that they are endowed by their Creator with certain unalienable Rights, that among these are Life, Liberty and the pursuit of Happiness.
—from the Declaration of Independence

This is Independence Hall, in Philadelphia, where the United States was born. Before 1776, it was the statehouse of Britain's Pennsylvania colony. Fighting between British soldiers and American revolutionaries had started in April 1775. But here on July 4, 1776, the members of the second Continental Congress signed the actual Declaration of Independence. Ever since, this place has been called Independence Hall. It is now part of Independence National Historical Park.

The Declaration of Independence was written mainly by Thomas Jefferson, with some help from other Founding Fathers, such as Benjamin Franklin and John Adams. It is one of the most, if not the single most, important work in all of American history, and one of the most important in world history. At its heart, and at the

Here, at Independence Hall, the Declaration of Independence was signed.

heart of the United States, is the belief that "all men are created equal," and that each has certain "unalienable" rights that assure freedom. That strong belief in freedom was new in its time. The victory of freedom in America helped pave the way for those who wanted freedom in many other lands. Later, "all men" came to mean "all people," including slaves and women as well as men. Many of these were still considered less than equal and without full rights when the Declaration of Independence was written.

Beside Independence Hall one can see the Liberty Bell. This was the great bell once located in Independence Hall, and was rung on July 8, 1776, with all of Philadelphia's bells, to celebrate the Declaration of Independence. The Liberty Bell was in regular use into the 1830s. It was cracked during Chief Justice John Marshall's funeral procession in 1835, but was rung as late as George Washington's birthday in 1846. Now it is protected by its own building, the Liberty Bell Pavilion, and is visited by hundreds of thousands of people every year.

At Independence Hall, in 1787, George Washington and the Continental Congress also wrote the Constitution, the document that provides the framework for the government of the United States of America. It, too, is one of the most important documents in American and world history. The Constitution and the Bill of Rights attached to it protect the freedoms that America's early revolutionaries fought for.

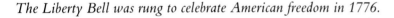

The Liberty Bell was rung to celebrate American freedom in 1776.

Inscription Rock

Later, about four hundred years ago, Spanish explorers and travelers arrived in the area. They, too, carved names and messages on Inscription Rock. One of the earliest to leave a name or message was Don Juan de Oñate. He was passing by in 1605, seven years after he came to New Mexico on his way back from the Gulf of California. Another early writer on the rock was Don Diego de Vargas. He reconquered New Mexico for Spain after the great Pueblo Revolt of the 1680s. Many other early Spanish and Mexican travelers, traders, and soldiers also carved their names and messages into the rock, as did many of the American pioneers who came later. Among them were many soldiers who went out to New Mexico during the Mexican-American War. A few years after that, gold seekers who were part of the great 1849 California gold rush felt the lure of Inscription Rock. So have many more Americans who have, since then, poured into the region. In a way, Inscription Rock holds a written record of the history of the Southwest.

Inscription Rock carries records of people going back centuries.

The impulse to carve a name or a message on a surface that will be visible to all who come upon it in the future goes far back in history. Here is one of the greatest examples of that in North America—Inscription Rock, also called El Morro National Monument.

Inscription Rock is a two-hundred-foot-high, flat-topped rock formation, called a mesa. It sits on a desert plateau seven thousand feet above sea level, in New Mexico. Old pueblos—Indian towns—also sit atop the mesa. They were built by the Zuñi people, who lived in them long before the Europeans came here. They and other early peoples left very old drawings, called petroglyphs, on Inscription Rock.

People have written in many languages and forms at Inscription Rock.

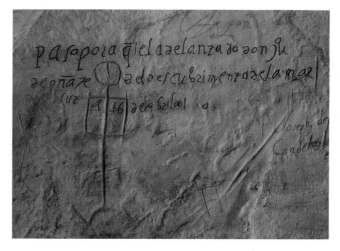

25

Jamestown

In 1607, three small sailing ships came to Jamestown. The ships were the *Susan Constant*, the *Goodspeed*, and the *Discovery*. They carried the colonists who founded the first successful English settlement in North America.

Jamestown is on the coast of southern Virginia, so these colonists faced no bitterly cold New England winter, as the Plymouth colonists would face thirteen years later. Even so, their first three years were terribly hard. In spite of the leadership of such colonists as Captain John Smith, they nearly gave up and went back home to England. But Lord Delaware brought them fresh supplies in 1610, and they decided to stay. Then, in 1612, colonist John Rolfe figured out how to grow tobacco and send it back for sale in England. The subsequent tobacco trade gave the people of Jamestown the means to support themselves.

During the early years the settlers at Jamestown were helped very much by their neighbors, the local Indians. When John Rolfe married an Indian woman named Pocahontas, daughter of Chief Powhatan, the two groups became even closer. As the settlement grew, however, it took more Indian land. After Powhatan's death, Indian discontent grew. In 1622, heavy Indian attacks took the lives of about 350 settlers. But the colony survived and continued to grow. Until 1699, it served as the capital of the Virginia colony.

Because it was first, Jamestown had some "firsts" among the English colonies. One of them — and nothing to be proud of — was that at Jamestown, in 1619, the first Black African slaves were brought to North America. Yet, in that same year, the Virginia House of Burgesses was formed. The House of Burgesses was the first elected governing body in the colonies, and represents the start of the long road to the Continental Congress and the start of the United States. And that is a very big "first" indeed.

Early settlers in Jamestown lived in houses something like these.

L'Anse aux Meadows

Flowers grow on the roof of this sod hut at L'Anse aux Meadows.

Once, long ago, L'Anse aux Meadows was a small Viking settlement. It lies far north in what is now Canada, on the northern tip of the province of Newfoundland. It does not look like much now—just eight little huts. Archeologists have dug these huts out of mounds of earth—mounds that had built up around them for almost one thousand years.

But this settlement is very important indeed. For a long time, until L'Anse aux Meadows was found, an argument raged about who actually "discovered" America. We knew that Norse Vikings from Scandinavia had settled in Iceland about twelve hundred years ago. And we knew that, led by Erik the Red, some had gone on to settle in Greenland, about one thousand years ago. But we did not know whether they had

also come to the mainland of North America. Erik the Red's son, Leif Eriksson, was said to have traveled to a place called Vinland. This place was thought to be in North America. But there was no hard proof of Viking settlements on the mainland.

Then, in 1960, Helge Ingstad and George Decker discovered the Viking settlement at L'Anse aux Meadows. In the buildings there, they found many things, including a Viking stone oil lamp, knitting needles, rivets, wood from the Norse shipwright's workshop, and slag from the Norse metal furnaces. The argument over who had "discovered" America was over. The Vikings had come to North America and lived there hundreds of years before Columbus arrived.

Lexington and Concord

The "shot heard 'round the world" was fired not far from the Old North Bridge.

The American Revolution began in the towns of Lexington and Concord, near Boston, Massachusetts. Boston had long been a center of resistance to British rule in the American colonies. There were many key events that led to the decision to break away from British rule. Among them were the following: In 1770, five Americans, including black freedman Crispus Attucks, were killed by British troops on Boston Common, an event that was later called the Boston Massacre. In 1773, the Sons of Liberty—one of them Paul Revere—dumped British tea into Boston Harbor to protest British taxes against Americans. This was the famous Boston Tea Party. By 1775, thousands of British troops had occupied Boston. And thousands of Americans in and around Boston had armed themselves, expecting the Revolution to come.

On the night of April 18, 1775, about seven hundred British troops secretly marched out of Boston toward Lexington and Concord, looking for stores of American arms. But their march turned out to be no secret, for the Americans were ready for them. Paul Revere had arranged to signal their coming from the belfry of Old North Church in Boston. His signal was "one if by land, two if by sea." That is, one lantern shining from the church meant that the British were marching by land, while two lanterns meant they were coming by ship. He signaled that the British were crossing the Charles River in boats. Then he, Dr. Samuel Prescott, William Dawes, and others rode out into the countryside, warning that the British were coming. Paul Revere was captured by the British, but the others got through. This has come to be known as Paul Revere's Ride.

By the time the British troops reached Lexington, about seventy armed Americans were waiting for them. These were the minutemen, soon to become part of the new American army. Someone, British or American, fired a first shot, and the British troops then fired on the Americans, killing eight and wounding ten.

The British next moved on to Concord, where they faced a larger force of four hundred minutemen, with more Americans gathering fast. At Old North Bridge in Concord, the British and Americans fought the first battle of the American Revolution. A few soldiers were killed on each side. The British held Concord for a short time, but by noon they began retreating toward Lexington and Boston on a road that was later called Battle Road. During that retreat, the British lost many soldiers, as the Americans fired on them from both sides. The British force might have been destroyed, but one thousand more British troops, with cannons, were sent out from Boston to support them. The combined British force then fought its way back to Boston, with heavy losses. The American Revolution had begun.

Much of this first revolutionary battleground, including Old North Bridge and Battle Road, is now part of Minute Man National Historic Park.

British and Americans fought their way along Battle Road.

Louisbourg

Soldiers in colonial dress at Louisbourg.

Louisbourg is a huge fortress on Canada's foggy North Atlantic coast. It is on the far eastern tip of Cape Breton Island, which is part of the Canadian province of Nova Scotia.

In 1719, when building of the fortress was started, Canada was called New France. The province of Nova Scotia was then called Acadia, and Cape Breton Island was the Isle Royale. At that time, France and Great Britain were deeply involved in a long series of wars over who would rule in North America, which ended with the conclusion of the French and Indian War, in 1760.

The French built Louisbourg intending it to be their main Atlantic fortress. By then they had

lost all of Newfoundland and much of Nova Scotia to the British. From Louisbourg, they hoped to establish control of the whole North Atlantic coast. Louisbourg was the base of a powerful French war fleet, which protected French ships traveling across the Atlantic. And Louisbourg's five-thousand-man garrison represented the largest French force in North America. French pirates based in Louisbourg attacked British and New England ships crossing the Atlantic or trading along the New England coast, and a big French fishing fleet was protected by Louisbourg, thereby protecting an industry that was important to both France and New France.

This huge stone fortress took a long time to

build. By 1745, some twenty-six years after it was begun, the French had almost finished it. But the French-British wars continued, and in that year, a British fleet and four thousand New England volunteers attacked and took Louisbourg. The British held it for three years, and then returned it to France as part of a larger peace treaty.

Although back in control of the fort, the French held Louisbourg for only ten more years. The long series of French-British wars in North America finally ended with a complete British victory. In 1758, a large British army and fleet attacked and took Louisbourg. Two years later, in 1760, the British completely destroyed the fortress, right down to the ground. They wanted it never again to be used by the French or anyone else. When they were done, only a grass-covered hill remained where the huge fortress had once stood.

And that is the way it stayed for 201 years, when, in 1961, the Canadian government, honoring Canada's French heritage, began to restore the site. It is now Canada's Fortress of Louisbourg National Historic Park. Some of Louisbourg's great buildings and walls have been rebuilt, as they were when it was a functioning fortress. Many of the over two million artifacts dug up at the site are now seen by the many visitors to this huge restoration.

The great fortress at Louisbourg was completely flattened in 1760.

Middleton Place

Middleton Place, in Charleston, South Carolina, has for over three hundred years been the home of the Middleton family. The Middletons were one of America's leading families in colonial times and during the American Revolution. Henry Middleton represented South Carolina at the first Continental Congress and became its president. Arthur Middleton, his oldest son, went to the second Continental Congress for South Carolina, in 1776, and was a signer of the Declaration of Independence.

Middleton Place also has some of the oldest and most beautifully landscaped gardens in the United States. They served as a model for many that were built later on. Henry Middleton began to create these gardens—including those shaped like a butterfly—in 1741. The gardens survived almost untouched, even during the Civil War, when much of the house itself was destroyed by the Union army. In the gardens stands the huge Middleton Oak, a tree more than one thousand years old. That tree was living and growing long before the Middletons—or for that matter Columbus—came to America.

This home and these gardens were also part of a large plantation, with many hundreds of slaves, before the Civil War ended slavery. In fact, the unfortunate side of the story is that it was built in part with the money made for its owners by their slaves. Williams Middleton, Henry's son, was one of those who, before the Civil War, led South Carolina to secede from the Union.

Middleton Place is famed for its butterfly gardens.

Monterey

Point Pinos lighthouse guided sailors into the port of Monterey.

Today, Monterey is a relatively small town on the California coast, just south of San Francisco. It is a lovely town, chiefly notable for its restored old buildings, good seafood restaurants, and fishing piers. It is also near the beginning of the long, beautiful Pacific-coast road that goes to Carmel, Big Sur, and then hundreds of miles south to Los Angeles.

Yet there was a time when Monterey was one of the most important towns in all of California. Over two hundred years ago, the new American nation was beginning its long drive west to the Pacific. At that time, Monterey was the capital of Spanish California, serving as an important outpost of Spain's huge American empire, which stretched all the way from northern California to the southern tip of South America.

Spanish explorer Juan Cabrillo sighted Monterey Bay when he sailed north along the California coast in 1546. But the first Spanish explorer to land there was Sebastián Vizcaíno, in 1602. Much later, in 1770, a party led by Catholic priest Junípero Serra and Captain Gaspar de Portolá reached Monterey by land. Father Serra set up a mission, which he soon moved to nearby Carmel. Governor de Portolá built his headquarters at Monterey, at a fort called the Presidio. From there, he and his soldiers ruled the area. So Monterey became the capital of Spanish California.

Among the many historic buildings in Old Monterey is the Royal Presidio Chapel, part of de Portolá's original Presidio, and now a national historic landmark. Monterey's old Custom House is an interesting sight, as is the lighthouse on Point Pinos, which once guided ships into Monterey Bay.

Monticello

Jefferson designed many unique features for his home, Monticello.

Monticello was the home of Thomas Jefferson, the extraordinary man who wrote the Declaration of Independence and was the third president of the United States. Jefferson's home stands on a hilltop in southern Virginia, looking out toward the Blue Ridge Mountains twenty miles away. Nearby is Shadwell, Virginia, where Jefferson was born in 1743.

Monticello means "little mountain" in Italian. Jefferson built the house in an Italian "classical revival" style, which was unusual for its time. Many of its features, like the dumbwaiters, which were small elevators pulled by ropes, remain as fine examples of Jefferson's ingenuity and creativity. Jefferson also had an unusual out-door-indoor weather vane, connected to the weather vane on his roof, but readable from inside. This was a very early device similar to the outdoor-indoor thermometers we have today.

Jefferson began clearing the land for Monticello in 1768, when he was only twenty-five years old. He began the house a year later, in 1769. A year after that, when his childhood home at Shadwell burned down, he moved in, but at that point, the house was far from finished. Actually, because of his patriotic involvement in the events surrounding the Revolution, Jefferson did not completely finish Monticello until thirty-nine years later, in 1809.

Mount Vernon

Washington spent most of his active life away from his home, Mount Vernon.

Mount Vernon was the home of George and Martha Washington. From here, he went out to lead his country to freedom—first as commander in chief during the American Revolution, and then as president. And when his work was done, he came home to Mount Vernon.

Mount Vernon was Washington's home for forty-five years, from 1754 until his death in 1799. Again and again over the years, he expanded the small house he started with, until he had completed the mansion that stands today.

Washington developed a large working plantation at Mount Vernon, growing mostly tobacco and wheat. There he employed about 240 people, some free people, but many slaves. Several revolutionary leaders, such as Benjamin Franklin, were active in the fight against slavery. Washington, though, was a slaveholder all his life. Although he did state that he was against slavery, and that he wanted his country to abolish it, his own slaves were freed only after his death.

Washington left Mount Vernon to fight in the French and Indian War and returned in 1758. The longest period of time he spent at Mount Vernon was from then to the beginning of the American Revolution, when he became commander in chief of the Continental Army. From then on, his life belonged to his country, rather than to his land and family. Right after the Revolution he became president. Only in 1797, after the end of his second presidential term, did Washington come home for good.

Today, Mount Vernon is one of America's most-visited places. Every year, over a million people come to see the home of the man who has—from the start—been called the Father of His Country.

Paul Revere House

At Lexington and Concord, in 1775, the American Revolution began when the British marched out of Boston, toward Lexington, in search of American weapon-storage sites. The Americans were warned they were coming by Paul Revere, who had set up the signal—two lanterns, high in the bell tower of Boston's Old North Church—and then, with William Dawes and Dr. Samuel Prescott, rode out to warn the Americans that the British were coming.

In our history books, that is Paul Revere's Ride, though it belonged just as much to Dawes and Prescott. We know Paul Revere best for that ride and the lanterns in the bell tower. But Paul Revere was an active American patriot long before the Revolution and is remembered for other things as well. He was one of the finest silver-smiths of his time, and to this day, his work is admired and shown in many museums and private collections. He was a political cartoonist, too. His best-known cartoon, drawn after the Boston Massacre, showed the British troops firing on unarmed Americans.

Paul Revere was very active in the American cause. From 1770 on through the Revolution, he carried messages for Boston's revolutionaries throughout the northern colonies. In 1773, he helped dump British tea into Boston Harbor at the Boston Tea Party. He also made gunpowder and cannons for the American army. After the war, he went into several different businesses but was still mainly a silversmith. In Boston, Paul Revere's house has been preserved, to honor this early patriot.

The house of Paul Revere, the "midnight rider," still stands in Boston.

Plains of Abraham

The British climbed up behind fortified Quebec to surprise the French.

Here, in Quebec City, Canada, is the final great battlefield of the French and Indian War— and thus it marks the final British-French battle for control of North America. The battlefield is the Plains of Abraham. Here a British army led by General James Wolfe defeated a French army led by the Marquis de Montcalm. After this battle, the city of Quebec and soon all of New France—French Canada—fell to the British.

Quebec City was the capital and greatest city of New France. The city sits on a great rock formation overlooking the St. Lawrence River, near what was once the Huron village of Stadacona. French explorer Jacques Cartier passed Stadacona when he moved south along the St. Lawrence in 1535. Samuel de Champlain set up a trading post there in 1608 and built Quebec's first fort, Fort St. Louis, in 1620.

Quebec City was the center of French strength in North America. But it was also always a city frequently at war, or close to war, with the British. Only nine years after Champlain built his fort, British troops attacked and took it, but then left. A New England fleet and troops attacked it again in 1690, but were held off. A British fleet was wrecked in the St. Lawrence River on its way to attack Quebec in 1711.

In 1759, the French and British were at war all over the world, in the Seven Years War. Part of this conflict was a struggle for control of North America, called the French and Indian War. That spring, a strong British fleet and army came into the St. Lawrence River and again attacked Quebec.

The British spent all summer trying to take Quebec, but could find no way up the great cliffs to the French fortress commanding the city. On the night of September 12, 1759, they finally found a pathway and secretly moved their whole army up to the top of the hill on the French side of the river. The surprised French found the British on the Plains of Abraham the next morning, ready to fight.

The battle itself then only took a few minutes. The experienced British regular troops stood their ground under French fire. The French, mostly volunteers, charged, lost many men, and then gave way and quickly lost the battle. General Wolfe was wounded in those few minutes, and died on the Plains of Abraham. The Marquis de Montcalm was wounded, too, and died the next day. Within a year of that brief battle the British controlled all of what had been New France.

Today, the Plains of Abraham is included in the National Battlefields of Quebec National Historic Park. Every year, it is visited by hundreds of thousands of Canadians—and many Americans, too. Quebec City is now the capital of the Canadian province of Quebec.

On Quebec's Plains of Abraham, the French lost North America.

Plymouth Rock

At Plymouth Rock, the Pilgrims began to create a new society.

Plymouth, Massachusetts, is one of the most significant and well-known historical sites in America. It was there that the Pilgrims landed, in 1620, to found the first New England colony. The colony was named after Plymouth, England, from where they had sailed across the sea to America. The Pilgrims came to America seeking freedom to practice their Puritan religion, which objected to many of the practices of the Church of England. They paved the way for the millions of others who have come to America seeking freedom since then.

The ship they sailed on, the *Mayflower*, was a tiny ship, only about ninety feet long and about twenty-six feet wide at its widest. The Pilgrims had started out from Southampton, England, in two ships, the *Speedwell* and the *Mayflower*. But the *Speedwell* proved unfit to cross the ocean and was left at Plymouth, where some of the Pilgrims also decided to stay in England. The rest boarded the *Mayflower* and set sail for America. On September 16, 1620, the *Mayflower* left Plymouth carrying 101 Pilgrims, 20 to 30 crew members, and Captain Christopher Jones. It was a long, hard trip across the ocean in that "nutshell" of a ship. At Plymouth today there is a full-size replica of the *Mayflower*, named the *Mayflower II*. Visitors can see for themselves just how tiny the *Mayflower* really was, and how hard the journey must have been. It was especially hard because the prevailing winds and currents in the North Atlantic run from west to east—from America to England. So ships sailing to America have to go against the wind and current all the way. Later, steamships had little trouble with wind and current. But in early times, it often took twice as long and was much rougher to cross from Europe to America than to go the other way.

On November 21, 1620, the Pilgrims landed first at what is now Provincetown, at the tip of Cape Cod. They had been at sea for two months, and there were still 101 Pilgrims on board. Although one person had died on the way, one baby had also been born. The Pilgrims stayed at Provincetown for a month, looking for a place to settle. While in Provincetown, they wrote the Mayflower Compact. This important agreement stated the idea of political equality for the first time on American soil. Then, on December 26, they sailed the *Mayflower* into Plymouth Harbor, where they finally settled.

Plymouth Rock itself is not very big, and it looks even smaller sitting inside the large shelter built for it at the foot of Coles Hill, at Plymouth Harbor. Actually, the rock used to be a little bigger, but—before it was protected—people chipped away at it for souvenirs, diminishing the landmark that honors the Pilgrims and the idea of freedom they brought to America.

Pilgrims crossed the Atlantic in a ship much like the modern Mayflower II.

Point Loma

The lighthouse on Point Loma marks the entrance to San Diego Bay.

Yet Cabrillo was not seeking what he actually found. Like so many other early explorers of North America, he was looking for an easier route from Europe to the riches of China and the rest of East Asia. He wanted to find a passage by water from the Atlantic to the Pacific. Instead, he found a new part of North America.

Cabrillo and his sailors went ashore at San Diego. Although they were attacked by Indians, they explored the area, including Point Loma. Then they returned to their ships and moved on up the coast. The sailors sighted many landmarks and made several landings on their way north. Cabrillo himself did not live to see them all. He died on the way, at San Miguel Island, in 1543. But his ships continued north and went as far as what is now southern Oregon before turning toward home.

Today, the United States Navy occupies much of Point Loma and the fine harbor of San Diego. On Point Loma itself stands the old San Diego Lighthouse. There, too, is the Cabrillo National Monument, honoring Juan Cabrillo, who discovered California.

Juan Cabrillo discovered Point Loma in 1542.

In 1542, just fifty years after Columbus came to America, Spanish explorer Juan Rodríguez Cabrillo discovered the coast of what is today California. In that year, his two little ships, the *San Salvador* and the *Victoria*, sailed north along the Mexican coast. When he reached Point Loma, Cabrillo sailed into a wide harbor he called San Miguel Bay. Today this is San Diego Bay, a great harbor filled with thousands of ships of all sizes. Then, 450 years ago, it was an unknown place. Cabrillo had made a great discovery.

Port Royal

This is Canada's oldest existing settlement and a key place in Canadian history. Port Royal, on the coast of Nova Scotia, was settled by the French in 1605, fifteen years before the Pilgrims came to Plymouth, farther south on the Atlantic coast of North America.

French explorers Samuel de Champlain and Sieur Pierre de Monts came to Port Royal, where they built a small fort and called it The Habitation. Soon, a settlement began to build up in and around the fort. Three years later, Champlain built a similar small fort at Quebec City, and also named that The Habitation. That little fort at Quebec was to become the center of French power in Canada.

But The Habitation at Port Royal, in the French province of Acadia, did not grow strong. From the start, it was a battlefield in the British-French fight for North America. In 1613, it was destroyed by British ships from Virginia. In 1635, the French built a new fort nearby, at Annapolis Royal, which France and Britain fought over for another century. From 1667 until 1710, when the British finally took most of French Acadia, Annapolis Royal was the capital of Acadia. Then, for another thirty years, it was the capital of Nova Scotia, as the British renamed Acadia.

Under British rule, Annapolis Royal was renamed Fort Anne, and is now Fort Anne National Historic Park. The Habitation at Port Royal has been restored, as Champlain first built it, and is now Port Royal National Historic Park.

The Habitation at Port Royal has been rebuilt for modern visitors.

Salem

The Custom House was at the center of old Salem's trading activity.

In the years after the Pilgrims came to Plymouth, sailors and settlers who came to New England began to build towns all along the New England coast. One of the earliest of these was Salem, about fifteen miles north of Boston. It was settled in 1626, just six years after Plymouth, and grew to be one of America's most important early port cities.

For over two hundred years, Salem's ships sailed the seas all over the world. Out of Salem sailed a large part of New England's fishing fleet, in pursuit of cod and herring in the stormy North Atlantic, and whales there and in more distant seas. Out of Salem also sailed much of New England's trading fleet. These ships brought back silk, spices, fine artwork, and much more from China and all East Asia. They also brought back rum from the islands of the Caribbean and, for some years, slaves from Africa.

In the late 1600s, Salem was also noted for having a huge witchcraft scare—literally a witch-hunt. It was led by Puritan minister Cotton Mather, and resulted in a series of trials of accused "witches." By the time it was all over, hundreds of people had been arrested, and twenty had been executed.

During the American Revolution, Salem's sailors fought the British, either as privateers who attacked British merchant ships or as seamen in America's small new navy. After the war, Salem was one of the new country's busiest seaports, competing successfully, for a time, with Boston and other such very large seaports, which later dominated America's trade.

Part of Salem's old waterfront area is now preserved as a national historic site.

Santa Fe

Pueblo and Apache, Yankee and Mexican, Missouri trader and great Spanish landowner—all met here, at the Palace of the Governors in historic Santa Fe.

This is the oldest government building in the United States. It was built in 1610 on Santa Fe's old central Plaza by Pedro de Peralta, Spanish governor of New Mexico. Santa Fe has been a capital city for the region ever since, first as part of colonial Spain, then as part of Mexico, and later as capital of the state of New Mexico. For a short time, in the late 1600s, Santa Fe was also the headquarters of the great Pueblo Indian revolt that drove the Spanish out of New Mexico for a few years.

Santa Fe—the name is Spanish for "Holy Faith"—is quite naturally the capital of New Mexico. As the major trading city of the old Southwest, it lay at the northern end of the old Chihuahua Trail, coming north from Mexico City. It also marked the western end of the Santa Fe Trail, which carried Americans from St. Louis and the Mississippi River into the Southwest. The Santa Fe Trail was one of the great pioneer trails that opened up the American West—the trail of the westbound wagon trains, and of Kit Carson and all the other mountain men. At Santa Fe, both trails met. So did the ancestors of the people who now live in the American Southwest.

The Palace of the Governors and the Plaza have been preserved for Santa Fe's many visitors. Nearby is San Miguel Mission, which was built in the 1600s and is the oldest church still in use in the United States.

The San Miguel Mission is the oldest United States church still in use.

Saratoga

Modern "soldiers" relive the 1777 Battle of Saratoga.

The Battle of Saratoga, in northern New York State, was one of the greatest American victories of the Revolutionary War. At Saratoga, in 1777, the American army trapped and captured General "Gentleman Johnny" Burgoyne's whole British army of over nine thousand men.

Had the battle gone the other way, the British might have won the war. The British goal was to cut New England off from the rest of the country, in the belief that they could then easily defeat the two separated parts. To do this, they planned to send Burgoyne's army south from Canada, an even larger army north from New York City, and a smaller British-Iroquois army from the west, along the Mohawk Valley. All three armies were to meet at Albany, in the center of the colony of New York. Victory then would have cut the colonies in two.

What happened instead was quite different.

First, the British and Iroquois coming from the west were stopped by General Nicholas Herkimer's army of frontiersmen at the Battle of Oriskany, near what is now Rome, New York. Then General William Howe's large British army in New York failed to move north along the Hudson River, even though they could have done so very easily. Burgoyne's army did come south out of Canada, but, without the help of the other two forces, found itself facing a much stronger American army. Seeing this, Burgoyne began to retreat. But at Saratoga, Burgoyne's army was encircled by twenty thousand American troops and surrendered without much of a fight.

The battlefield at Saratoga is now part of Saratoga National Historical Park, which covers four square miles of land beside the Hudson River, north of Albany.

Sitka

Today, Sitka is an American city on Baronof Island, just off the coast of Alaska. But for over 150 years, Sitka was a Russian city named New Archangel, and it was the capital of Russian America.

While Columbus and others were sailing west to explore America, Russian explorers were moving east across Asia to the Pacific. When they reached the eastern tip of Asia, it was only a short distance across the Bering Strait to Alaska and the rest of North America. To reach America, they just hopped from island to island until they reached the mainland of Alaska. By the mid-1700s, Russians were exploring Alaska and the Pacific coast of North America.

In 1799, an expedition headed by Alexander Baronof landed at what is now Sitka, where he built Fort St. Michael. From this fort, Russians trapped and traded with the local Tlingit people for sea otter furs, which were worth a great deal when brought to China. The Russian people also trapped and traded for other furs and continued to explore south along the North American coast.

Three years after it was built, the Tlingits destroyed Fort St. Michael and killed most of the Russian settlers there. But two years after that, Baronof returned with a much stronger force. This time he defeated the Tlingits and founded the city of New Archangel, which became the capital of Russian America two years later.

New Archangel grew rapidly and remained the capital of Russian America until the United States bought Alaska from Russia in 1867. The city, renamed Sitka, was also the capital of the Territory of Alaska for many years. The site of the Russian-Tlingit battle is now a national historic park.

As New Archangel, Sitka was capital of Russian Alaska.

Taos Pueblo

Towns like Taos Pueblo were built long before the Spanish came.

In the American Southwest, the Anasazi Indians—their name means "the Old Ones"—still live in towns, or pueblos, their people built long before Columbus discovered the New World.

One of the most fascinating of these old towns is Taos Pueblo, in New Mexico, about seventy miles north of Santa Fe. To this day, over a thousand Pueblo Indians live in Taos, and their people have lived there since long before the Spanish conquerors invaded their land in the 1500s. One Spanish explorer—Hernando de Alvarado, an officer in the expedition through the Southwest led by Francisco Vasquéz de Coronado—visited Taos in 1540. Another—Don Juan de Oñate—came to the area with two hundred settlers in 1598 and stayed.

Subsequently Taos Pueblo became a center of Pueblo Indian resistance to Spanish rule. In 1680, the people of Taos led a powerful revolt against the Spanish, killing over four hundred Spanish settlers. They forced the rest—about twenty-two hundred people—to flee south across the Rio Grande, the river that today forms part of the border between the United States and Mexico. But the Pueblo Indians' freedom lasted only thirteen years, until 1693, when strong Spanish forces retook the area. This time they stayed and held it for over 150 years.

There were other Pueblo revolts over the centuries, but none succeeded. In 1847 one of them occurred during the Mexican-American War, when Taos was occupied by American forces. After the war, the United States took much of the Southwest from Mexico, including Taos Pueblo. American frontiersman Kit Carson was an Indian agent in Taos during the 1850s.

At times, as many as twenty-five hundred people have lived in Taos Pueblo. There are fewer of them now. But the people of Taos Pueblo have survived it all. So has their great Taos Fair, dating back to early Spanish times. It draws tens of thousands of visitors every year.

Touro Synagogue

Newport's Touro Synagogue is the oldest in the nation.

Touro Synagogue, in Newport, Rhode Island, is the oldest active Jewish house of worship in the United States, dating back to 1763.

Like most Americans, Jews came to America for freedom and opportunity. In Newport, they found both. Early Rhode Island settlers, including the colony's founder, Roger Williams, believed strongly in religious and political freedom. So when a group of Spanish-Portuguese Jews came here in 1658, they were welcomed.

The Jewish community in Newport grew slowly at first. But in the 1740s a new law made it easier for Jews to become full citizens. Soon many more Jews came to America. By the 1760s, the Jewish community at Newport was ready to build its own house of worship, and the Touro Synagogue was the result.

By the time of the American Revolution, there were an estimated 1,000 American Jews out of Newport's 8,000 to 9,000 people. Newport was at that time the largest Jewish community in the new United States, though there were also substantial Jewish communities in New York City, Philadelphia, and Charleston, and smaller communities throughout the country. New York's Jewish community was the oldest, having been established in 1654, when New York was still Dutch New Amsterdam.

The Jews of Newport were mostly merchants, who made and sold whale-oil candles, built ships, and traded in rum, tobacco, slaves, and much else. One of the best-known of them was the merchant Aaron Lopez, who in 1759 laid the first of the six cornerstones of the Touro Synagogue.

Valley Forge

Washington and von Steuben created a new army at Valley Forge.

For George Washington's Continental army, the hard winter spent at Valley Forge was nearly a disaster. Yet, despite significant losses, the army of revolutionaries came out of it better able to fight and win the war.

Going into Valley Forge, it all looked very bad indeed. It was December 1777. The British held New York and Philadelphia. The less-experienced Americans had been beaten in battles at Brandywine and Germantown. They had very little food and no warm winter clothing. Their only shelters were the nine hundred unheated little huts the soldiers had managed to put together on arrival at Valley Forge. Many soldiers were going home for the winter, to return in the spring. Many others were ready to desert and not come back at all.

As a very cold winter came on, conditions became worse. Of the soldiers who stayed, many became sick, and some died of their illnesses. If the strong, well-fed British army in nearby Philadelphia had attacked the Americans that winter, that might have been the end of Washington's army—and perhaps the Revolution, too. Of the eleven thousand men who camped at Valley Forge, only six thousand were left in the spring, although many then came back to fight the British.

But the British did not attack. Washington and his aide, Friedrich von Steuben, used the winter to train and drill the inexperienced American army. That winter, they created the heart of the Continental army. Six years later, their army—with the help of the French army and fleet—was able to win the war.

Williamsburg

The British colonial governor lived in Williamsburg at Governor's Palace.

At Williamsburg, one of the greatest American speakers of his time gave his greatest speech. The time was March 1775, less than a month before the American Revolution began at Lexington and Concord. The speaker was Patrick Henry, a member of Virginia's House of Burgesses, which was then meeting at Williamsburg. Addressing the House, he called for the revolution that was to come, with the now-famous lines ending his speech, "Give me liberty, or give me death!"

As the colonial capital of Virginia from 1699 to 1780, Williamsburg—like Boston—was at the heart of the events leading up to the American Revolution. Before the war, George Washington and Thomas Jefferson were also delegates to the House of Burgesses, as were many other Founding Fathers of the United States. Many of the beliefs and principles they brought to the emerging nation as a whole were first debated and discussed here.

Today, Williamsburg is history brought to life. Starting over sixty years ago, in 1926, much of the old town has been restored. Williamsburg is now much as it was in colonial times. Hundreds of restored buildings and gardens there make it by far the largest and most important of all the American restorations. Craftspeople in colonial dress work as early Americans once did. They, together with the original work of colonial craftspeople on display, help to bring Williamsburg to life for hundreds of thousands of visitors every year.

Many of those visitors also travel to nearby Jamestown and Yorktown. Together, these three places make up the Colonial National Historical Park.

Yorktown

The Revolutionary War ended in the Surrender Room at Moore House.

At Yorktown, in southern Virginia, in 1781, the final great battle of the American Revolution was fought and won. It was not a bloody battle. In fact, losses were light on both sides. But had the British won, there might be no United States today.

Victory came at a time when many Americans thought their cause was almost lost. By 1781, the war had been going on for six and a half long, long years, since Lexington and Concord. France had come into the war on the side of the Americans. But British forces were still far stronger than the combined American and French armies. In New York City alone, the British had an army of seventeen thousand troops facing an American army only half that

size, led by George Washington. In Virginia, over seven thousand British troops led by General Charles Cornwallis seemed about to cut the South off from the rest of the country.

But Washington and the French decided on a bold gamble that helped win the war. In May, the French sent a fleet of warships to Newport and forty-five hundred troops to reinforce Washington's army in the Hudson Valley, north of New York City. The French also promised to send another fleet and three thousand more troops in August.

Washington and the French then could have attacked the British army in New York. That is what the British expected them to do. Instead, Washington moved most of his American-French army south to trap the British southern army, dangerously leaving only a small force at West Point to defend the Hudson Valley. Washington's army met the combined French fleets and reinforcements in Maryland and proceeded by ship to Yorktown, Virginia. The combined American-French army, now fifteen thousand strong, attacked the much-smaller British army at Yorktown at the same time as the French fleet fought and defeated the British southern fleet, cutting off Cornwallis's escape.

Cornwallis had been promised a large British fleet and strong reinforcements from New York, and he prepared to hold out against the Americans and French. He dug in at Yorktown and waited. But the British waited too long before leaving New York, and just as their promised fleet was setting sail, Cornwallis ran out of time. On October 19, 1781, Cornwallis surrendered almost eight thousand British soldiers and sailors to Washington. As the British marched out to surrender to the Americans, the British army bands played a popular song of the time—"The World Turned Upside Down."

That final battle at Yorktown won the war. It took two years more for a peace treaty to be signed between the new United States and Great Britain. But after Yorktown there was no doubt about it: The new American nation had fought its way to freedom.

On a foggy October day, soldiers reenact the Battle of Yorktown.

Acknowledgments

We are grateful to Domenico Firmani for his always-expert help on this book. As photo researcher, he has reached out around North America and beyond for just the right pictures of these great American places. We also thank the many people and organizations who allowed us to use their photographs. Their names are detailed in the Photo Credits below.

We also very much appreciate the help of the people at the Chappaqua Library—Director Mark Hasskarl, the reference librarians, including Mary Platt, Paula Peyraud, Terry Cullen, Martha Alcott, and Carolyn Jones, and the whole circulation staff, among them Caroline Chojnowski, Jane McKean, and Marcia Van Fleet. They and the staff of Westchester's Interlibrary Loan System have been unfailingly helpful.

And, finally, thanks to our editor at Atheneum, Jonathan Lanman, and to our publisher, Judy Vantrease Wilson, for their support of this introduction to the historic places of early America.

Photo Credits

Photo Credit Abbreviations
NPS: National Park Service, U.S. Department of Interior
ECP: Environment Canada—Parks
DRIE: Department of Regional Industrial Expansion, Canada

p. iii: Middleton Place, T.R. Richardson; p. viii: NPS, Richard Frear; p. 2: California Office of Tourism; p. 3: San Diego CVB, California Office of Tourism; pp. 4–5: NPS, Fred E. Mang, Jr.; p. 6: NPS, Richard Frear; p. 7: NPS, Richard Frear; p. 8: NPS, Richard Frear; p. 9: NPS, M. Woodbridge Williams; pp. 10–11: NPS, Jack E. Boucher; p. 12: Puerto Rico Tourism Co.; p. 13: Puerto Rico Tourism Co., Meredith Pillon; p. 14: NPS, Richard Frear; p. 15: New York Convention and Visitors Bureau; p. 16: NPS, Richard Frear; p. 17: California Department of Parks and Recreation; p. 18: New York State Commerce Department; p. 19: Fraunces Tavern Museum; p. 20: NPS, Richard Frear; p. 21: ECP, Fred Cattroll; p. 22: Huronia Historical Park; pp. 23–24: NPS, Richard Frear; p. 25: NPS, Fred E. Mang, Jr.; p. 26: NPS, Richard Frear; p. 27: DRIE; pp. 28–29: NPS, Richard Frear; p. 30: DRIE; p. 31: ECP, Fred Cattroll; p.32: Middleton Place, T. R. Richardson; p. 33: Monterey Visitor and Convention Bureau; p. 34: Virginia Division of Tourism; p. 35: Virginia Division of Tourism; p. 36: NPS; p. 37: ECP, P. St. Jacques; p. 38: ECP, Fred Cattroll; pp. 39–40: Plimoth Plantation; p. 41: NPS, Fred E. Mang, Jr.; p. 42: ECP, Jamie Steeves; p. 43: NPS, Richard Frear; p. 44: New Mexico Tourism and Travel Division, Mark Nohl; p. 45: NPS, Richard Frear; p. 46: Alaska Division of Tourism; p. 47: New Mexico Tourism and Travel Division, Mark Nohl; p. 48: NPS, Richard Frear; p. 49: NPS, Richard Frear; p. 50: Domenico G. Firmani; pp. 51–52: NPS Richard Frear

INDEX